W9-ARF-438

AUGUSTA SAVAGE

AUGUSTA SAVAGE

The Shape of a Sculptor's Life

MARILYN NELSON

Afterword by TAMMI LAWSON

Christy Ottaviano Books

LITTLE, BROWN AND COMPANY

New York Boston

Text copyright © 2022 by Marilyn Nelson
Afterword copyright © 2022 by Tammi Lawson

Cover art copyright © 2022 by Tatyana Fazlalizadeh. Interior design by Neil Swaab.
Cover copyright © 2022 by Hachette Book Group, Inc.

Hachette Book Group supports the right to free expression and the value of copyright. The purpose
of copyright is to encourage writers and artists to produce the creative works that enrich our culture.

The scanning, uploading, and distribution of this book without permission is a theft of the author's
intellectual property. If you would like permission to use material from the book (other than for review
purposes), please contact permissions@hbgusa.com. Thank you for your support of the author's rights.

Christy Ottaviano Books
Hachette Book Group
1290 Avenue of the Americas, New York, NY 10104
Visit us at LBYR.com

First Edition: January 2022

Christy Ottaviano Books is an imprint of Little, Brown and Company. The Christy Ottaviano
Books name and logo are trademarks of Hachette Book Group, Inc.

The publisher is not responsible for websites (or their content) that are not owned by the publisher.

All images reprinted with permission from the following sources: Michael Rosenfeld Gallery
LLC, New York, NY; Photographs and Prints Division, Schomburg Center for Research in Black
Culture, New York Public Library, Astor, Lenox and Tilden Foundations; Art and Artifacts
Division, Schomburg Center for Research in Black Culture, New York Public Library, Astor, Lenox
and Tilden Foundations; The Miriam and Ira D. Wallach Division of Art, Prints and Photographs:
Photography Collection, New York Public Library; Manuscripts and Archives Division, New York
Public Library, Astor, Lenox and Tilden Foundations; Knaust family collection, Saugerties, NY.
See photography credits on page 112 for more information.

Library of Congress Cataloging-in-Publication Data
Names: Nelson, Marilyn, 1946– author. | Lawson, Tammi, other.
Title: Augusta Savage : the shape of a sculptor's life / Marilyn Nelson ; afterword by Tammi Lawson.
Description: New York : Little, Brown and Company, 2022. | Summary: "A powerful biography
in poems about Augusta Savage, the trailblazing artist and pillar of the Harlem Renaissance—
with an afterword by the curator of the Schomburg Center for Research in Black Culture."
—Provided by publisher.
Identifiers: LCCN 2021030799 | ISBN 9780316298025 (hardcover) | ISBN 9780316298223 (ebook)
Subjects: LCSH: Savage, Augusta, 1892–1962—Poetry. | Sculptors—United States—Poetry. |
African American sculptors—Poetry. | Biographical poetry. | LCGFT: Pattern poetry.
Classification: LCC PS3573.A4795 A94 2022 | DDC 811/.54—dc23
LC record available at https://lccn.loc.gov/2021030799

ISBNs: 978-0-316-29802-5 (hardcover), 978-0-316-29822-3 (ebook)

Printed in the United States of America

LSC-C

Printing 1, 2021

For Tovah Antonia and Navah Salette
—MN

To my parents, James Oliver and Helen Marie Vance
—TL

CONTENTS
List of Poems

SECTION I 1892–1930

SECTION II 1931–1940

SECTION III 1941–1962

AUGUSTA SAVAGE

There are years that ask questions
and years that answer.

—ZORA NEALE HURSTON (1891–1960)

SECTION I

1892–1930

Portrait of a Baby

Leap-Year Baby

Augusta Christine Fells, 2/29/1892

Born on a date that in most years doesn't exist—
the only recluse of the calendar—
born on the bonus day, the extra day,
that falls every fourth year, for some reason
most people can't explain or understand.
To age by leap years, one to every four
years aged by ordinary people who
sprint toward their end. A leaper's free to choose
to celebrate on February twenty-eighth,
or March first, or February twenty-ninth,
thus choosing how old, how special, to be.
Leap-year babies believe they are unique.
They know they're born to make something happen.
But all of us are born knowing that. Right?

First Duckling

Gus Fells, 1898

from squish
to a formable ball,
     head, body
wings, tail, feathers detailed by fingernails,
and to the pond-seeing eyes, the slightly smiling beak
coming closer and closer to a heartbeat in the caught
breath of a colored girl who feels like God

Fifth Duckling

Did the Creator make
practice ducklings, too, on
the fifth day, like I'm going to til I
know they could almost paddle
and quack in the thick black puddle
on the far side of the clothesline behind our house? Did the
Creator make mistakes and have to squeeze a try back into dirt you better
not get on your pinafore, or I'll have to make you cut me a switch? Pa say only man
make mistakes, not God. He say God perfect. But why God made our people
been slaves, I want to know? And why He lets so many white mens fought on
the wrong side in the slavery war? Why He lets us some nights lay awake
with growly guts? Sometime I ask questions Pa say ain't no answers to.
But God, Pa say, makes no mistakes. He made heaven and earth right
in just one try, only six days out of dark emptiness, just by saying
some let there be's with His love, and then calling it good.

Garden Figure

Birth Order

Augusta, born seventh of fourteen

The firstborn child is a perfectionist.
The second child is a people-pleaser.
The third child is a little hellion.
The fourth child feels somehow different.

The fifth child is a perpetual sidekick.
The sixth child seethes with secret rebellion.
The seventh child is beaten for making art.
The eighth child wins the blue ribbon for charm.

The ninth is shy; the tenth an extrovert.
The eleventh child can disappear at will.
The seventh child is beaten for making art.
The twelfth and thirteenth children are a set.

The fourteenth child is the baby for eighty years.
The seventh child is beaten for making art.

The Figure of a Frog

for Augusta Savage

A figure of a frog is not a frog.
Nor are sticks carved into tree shapes
forests cleansing the air of our breath.
No more than a drawing or a painting on
sheepskin, paper, canvas, or a deep black
cave wall truly replicates animals fleeing men.
No more than words describing how gently light
strokes the live oak's leaves hanging over glad
chickens, words in a girl's hand, hidden under a
corn-shuck-stuffed mattress shared with three
of her sisters not because they are secret but
because they arose straight from the heart, let's
say, no more are those words an actual tree.
Some things are art, some things are poetry.
It's not likeness, but reverence,
Reverend Fell,
that makes an
image an idol.
Your Gussie's
clay figurines
were not made
to be idolized.
That was far
from the mind
of the little girl
who shaped
them carefully
of mud and wonder.

Wildfire

The child made tiny somethings from pinches
of the clay she found right in the backyard.
Enough ducklings for a duckling parade,
enough little bunnies and mice to bring
the other children to squeals of delight.
A large family of small laughing pigs.
Banjo-playing, fiddling, cakewalking dogs.
But the God of her father sent Moses
down from the mountain with that Thou Shalt Not
against making images. Her father's
fear of his God drove him to search for her
secret hiding places, to cut switches,
to beat the living daylights of art's sin
out of her, a man beating back wildfire.

Girl with Pigtails

Fingers Remember

Long	fing-	ers,	how
signals	flow	up	them
from	tip	and	finger-
print	all	the	way
up	the	arm	and
the	neck	to	what-
ever	magic	light	takes
flame	so	touch	ignites
as the	palm	smooths	warm

from one person to another, passes
sunlight one skin has taken in, which
the other receives like thirsty soil gulps
rain and infinite generations of ancestors
yawn awake asking if it's time for the line
to   miracle up a new life. They were so young,
and   innocence is a birth gift intended all along
to be   opened with love, promises, and blessing,
as you enter the future that only exists if you live
into it. His name was John. His moving muscles
formed shapes she had not met before. Green
time laid its fragranced landscape before them.
So they entered. Married. Irene came soon.
At eighteen, Gussie was widowed, with a
toddler older than her youngest siblings.
The family's hand opened and closed
in welcome. But fingers remember.

No Clay

While the Whole White World was at war
the Fellses grabbed the golden ring
of opportunity and moved
lock, stock, barrel, kit and caboodle
a few steps up to West Palm Beach.
There was a colored high school there, and jobs.
Gussie went back to school. Studied,
learned. Peace reigned in her father's house.
Birth siblings and siblings-in-law,
nieces and nephews aplenty,
a table grace before each meal,
a nice young man to walk out with:
She was almost happy. Almost
forgot art, forgave the beatings.
But she could find no clay. No clay.

Strut, Miss Savage

What girl wouldn't marry a guy
with such a terrific name? Who,
given a choice, wouldn't toss off
her meh surname, like a wedding
bouquet, and become a Savage
from now on in? To choose her name,
and to create her own future,
to name herself herself, set free
of all of her past but the love.
Augusta Savage. Mrs. James
Savage. Mrs. Fierce. Mrs. Strong.
Miss Tiger with the secret smile,
in her own home, with her own man
who has vowed to love her daughter
as if she were his, and who stopped
the wagon at Chase Pottery
and waited while his wife ran in
to introduce herself, who jumped
out and ran to help her carry
the buckets of clay Mr. Chase
had given her. Me. Augusta
Savage. My new name, my true life.

Augusta Savage

Making

Before I knead, clay
is white canvas, empty page,
a night without dreams.

Little warming lump,
you look back out of my palm,
ask me for a face.

Shapes I remember
with the tips of my fingers
emerge, and confess.

The duckling parade
I made and Papa destroyed
is a circus now.

What the eyes can see
and what the fingers can feel,
oh, generous world!

As we make the tools
that will form our creation,
our work defines us.

Hot Dog

My first real artist's job: teaching
fellow students how to shape clay!
And getting paid a whole dollar a day!
Five dollars a week, and I'm teaching art!
This is something I'd like to get used to!
Getting paid to do what you love to do!
As they say—it's nice work, if you can get it!
Maybe my gift isn't a sin, a curse,
just another of God's back-assed blessings.
Well, hot dog, Jesus! Lord, I'm on my way!

Halo

✿

Virgin and Child, 1915

Hail, Mary,
of resplendent grace,
clay formed by my fingers,
head bowed to accept this
tough gift, having been made
the bridge between Creator Lord
and mortal existence, the lone human
made to bear magnificent bereavement,
to surrender everything, everything, both
the humbling joy of being chosen, and but
however in spite of that joy universe to feel
the oh my God pain, the pain, the going on
forever for always pain, immortal though the
body dies thousands of daily deaths and then
dies here in the flow of time through the moonless
dark I give breast to the babe I was promised would
bring about a new, different, undreamed, undreamable
something, a helpless wonder in my arms gulping from
me the milk of his aloneness, his one lonely death unique
as every death, which was born from me with him on the
clean straw floor in air warmed by the breathing of the
uncomprehending animals, comprehending as little as I,
as we, sitting under the beautiful impersonal stars, do,
stars which stitch our permanent destinies to the sky,
as we ask all of them, every single star, why we are
forsaken and abandoned, nailed here to the pain we
can't share, can't share even with our own mothers,
who would bow to it, suffer it, die of it for us if
they could, as a mother would take her son's pain,
her son's weeping, his weeping, his weeping, her
son's weeping, my son, my son, my God, why.

Forgive Me, Baby

Gussie's father kneels,
holding his hat in his hands.
He says words she's waited for.

The Du Bois Commission

College wasn't my cup of tea.
And neither was my husband, James.
But I kept the name and made art.
My pieces won a blue ribbon
at the 1919 State Fair,
which led to commissions of busts
of local Negro notables,
a letter of introduction
to the sculptor Solon Borglum,
and the New York, New York–bound train.
I took a valise, the letter,
bade fond farewell to my daughter,
arrived with $4.60 and wide-eyed faith.
Got a job walking around with
a mop and bucket. Mr. Borglum
said, "Apply to Cooper Union."
So I did. And was admitted,
was given scholarship support.

I earned my high school diploma
and completed the four-year course
in three years, while working full-time
and studying African art
at the 135th Street branch
of the New York Public Library
in Harlem, where the Renaissance
was raging like a Mardi Gras.
Fine Yoruba sculptures, bronzes

19

from the Kingdom of Benin,
how my fingers yearned to touch them.
This Du Bois commission happened
because the librarian knew
somebody who knew somebody.
Now I build, petal by petal
on the armature, the broad, high brow,
the hooded eyes, arched nose, unsmiling cheeks,
the dapper, twirl-ended mustache,
the combed goatee, the hard, proud mouth:
a Negro leader made of moist clay.

Lenox Avenue

Harlem, Africa

Harlem attracts and births the "New Negro."
Amalgam of many Black cultures: the
Rural and urban American South,
Little sunny islands . . . People only
Emancipated some fifty years ago.
Many of us just learning how to dream.

Art, a lonely and a communal dream,
Feeds our developing identity,
Race the deep, flowing spring at its center.
"I'm Black," we say, now authentically proud.
Color's a medal meaning "I survived,
And now I'm here to kick the white man's butt."

(However, that's only a metaphor.)
All these writers and painters. "The Harlem
Renaissance," they call us, we young gifted
Lights lit to lead the race to true freedom.
Every one of us has something to prove.
May what we create make a difference.

A good rent party counts among its guests
Friends such as Langston, Zora, Claude McKay,
Ready to read new work. Dorothy West and
I plan to publish a journal of the arts.
Cleaning houses, taking in wash, I make
A meager living that I live for art.

How far I've come from Green Cove Springs. As if
All those Florida years weren't really *real*:
Real life is what you make of time, right now.
Lately, my sculptures seem to be trying to
Express what, essentially, the decade means.
What if my *The New Negro* winds up cast in bronze?

Within thirty seconds' walk of the 135th Street branch
of the New York Public Library

Marcus Garvey Sits for a Bust

Garvey in regalia

The Universal Negro Improvement Association,
he says, his little bloodshot eyes looking out
of the dark shadows of his overhanging black
brow. His eyebrows quizzical, halfway to a smile.
And over them, an uncreased expanse of dark brown
brain-cover, broad enough to maybe mean genius.
He talks and talks, a baritone that somehow lilts,
the Jamaican vowels a soothing music, talks and
talks, how we are Africans wherever we landed
in the genocidal kidnap, we belong to each
other as siblings, all Africa, all Africans, together
as one nation. We will return, we shall return, the
Motherland waits for us, she is calling to us in the drum
beats of our hearts, he says. Don't you hear it sometimes?
I have to say yes, I sure do sometimes, remembering how
sometimes I have smiled at insult and injustice, toed the
yassuh mister charley line. Don't forget a whole continent
hopes we will return with what we've learned, what we
have become, even our language, our words, even our
images, even our art, he says, is more theirs than ours. Light
falls from the windows through the antique lace curtains onto
a mahogany table set with his collection of antique porcelain.
His cheeks are silk sleek, his thick lips talking, talking,
the necessity of self-emancipation, only we can free our minds,
think about going home, feeling your Ancestors welcoming
you from the very soil. I place gray layers on the wire frame,
watching his face, watching my fingers. He gives off
black light, impossible to capture in my medium. Genius,
genius, yes, and authority. Confidence. And there's some
madness in there. I stroke the curves, the heavy jaw, the thick,
soft lips speaking hymns of affirmation. Something deep inside
me makes a little ding, like a tiny chime. My Black pride
has awakened. My cramped and crooked inner light
creaks straight. Those little eyes. That grand ambition.
I cover the bust with a damp cloth. Same time tomorrow?

Negress Denied Entry

It's nineteen-(censored)-twenty-three! You'd think
white people could treat us fairly by now!
My having been granted a scholarship—
a summer studying at Fontainebleau,
the school near Paris, center of the world
for artists—made a dream come true at last!
I'd been chosen by a group of artists!
I raised money to pay for the voyage,
bought a trunk, packed it with clothes and supplies.
Then got a note from the American
committee: My scholarship was withdrawn,
for fear that sailing with the likes of me
might offend white girls off to see gay Paree.

Hey, I know Garvey! My love is a Garveyite!
Robert's a writer for the *Negro World*!
I know a thing or two about the ways
those (censored) keep our people from success!
By God, I won't let them wreck my best chance!
I'll take my protest to the newspapers!
Famous Artists Draw Color Lines Against . . .
against ME. Shoot, I'm mad enough to spit!
Not just for my sake, but for the whole race,
for all of us denied opportunity!
How can you compete, when the (censored) (censored)
slam the (censored) door in your (censored) face?
Hell, better "a troublemaker" than erased!

Hitting Bottom

~~~~~~

R.I.P. Robert Poston (1891–1924) and Roberta Poston (1924):
husband and daughter of Augusta Savage

Our love still young,   our marriage new,
Robert and I   felt Blackness as
a second vow,   a spiritual seal
between two souls   who spent long years
before we met   wondering if
we would ever   find each other.
Now we were one   and would soon bring
a life into   being. A new
beautiful life,   a Black life,
we would love   and bring into the
Fells family.   Irene's sibling,
a new Negro beginning.
Robert left on assignment
to write about Liberia,
a foothold in the motherland.
He died at sea. Pneumonia.
The last letter he wrote to me
said Africa   doesn't want us.
Garvey was in   prison for fraud
(faked charges).   I was carrying
the child I wanted   to share with Robert.
Roberta came   early. Grief was
our midwife. God   must hate Negroes.
Why does God make   our luck so bad?
She lived ten days.   Is this the worst?
Is worse coming?   What is the point
of making art?   Flowers on graves?
Dancing in masks   to placate death?
I don't want it.   I don't want art.
Take the gift back.   With everything else.

Gallery Opening

Let me introduce myself to the most beautiful Negro girl I've ever seen.
I'm especially attracted to nut-brown girls like you, it's like a magnet. The
beauty of me, of course, is that I'm very rich. I'm Joe. Joseph Gould, named
for my grandfather, Doctor Joseph F. Gould, who was a surgeon during
the Civil War. After the war he delivered babies in Boston born with silver
spoons, and taught rich young men at Harvard Medical School. We Goulds
have been in America since the sixteen-thirties, a family of very superior
genes. We trace our line back to a twelfth-century knight. Goulds have
fought in every war in the history of the country; we're related to all the
best old New England families. My father, also a doctor, built my childhood
home in a Boston suburb called Norwood, on Washington Street, four
eighty-six Washington Street, three floors, twenty-one rooms, gables and
dormers and balconies and chestnut floors, and an eight-feet-tall mirror
decorated with gilded cherubim in the front hall. Fireplaces, diamond-
shaped varicolored windows on the landings. And there was I, a scrawny
little boy with a runny nose, a thorough disappointment to my father. At
thirteen I realized I was generally despised and laughed at, but I finished
school and went to Harvard, as was my birthright. There I met some people
and spent a few years debating what I should do with my life. I became a
fluent speaker of the language of sea gulls, translating some of the greatest
American poems into sea gull, glad to perform them at gatherings. My
favorite is the first few stanzas of "Hiawatha," which always causes a stir,
among both humans and gulls. But enough about me. I've been enamored
of Negroes since before I moved to New York. I became interested in the
subject of eugenics as a young man: so interested that I borrowed money
from my mother to take a summer course in eugenical fieldwork methods at
the Eugenics Record Office in Cold Spring Harbor, Long Island. After that
I borrowed a little more money from her and went out to North Dakota

to measure the heads of Indians. I measured the heads of five hundred Mandans and a thousand Chippewas, and then my money ran out. I hope you'll allow me to measure your head someday. My mother telegrammed me to return home at once, whereupon she told me that she and my father were in financial difficulties and had to sell our house. So I went to Boston and tried to raise money for another expedition to Indian reservations but was unsuccessful, and my father arranged a job for me in Norwood, where I used to like to wander around an old graveyard behind our house, where the weeds were waist high and I could lie down and hide and speculate on the rows on rows of skeletons lying on their backs in the dirt below, but I realized I had to move on. So I came to New York and landed in Greenwich Village, where I was at home among the dreamers and failures and the misfits and has-beens and the would-bes and the never-will-bes, and the God-knows-whats and the bums, with the idea of getting a job as a theater critic, because I thought that would leave me time to write the novels and plays and poems and songs and essays and an occasional scientific paper on some eugenical matter which I planned, and eventually I did succeed in getting a job as a messenger boy–slash–assistant reporter for the *Evening Mail*, and I was sitting on the back steps of Police Headquarters recovering from a hangover when I read in a book I had recently stolen from a secondhand bookstore a passage by William Butler Yeats, which stuck in my mind. I realized then and there that I am destined to write a book called "The Oral History of Our Time," which will contain every word I speak and hear, and every thought I have, during every waking minute of every day of the rest of my life. And this cerebral explosion made me see that I couldn't possibly continue to hold down a job, because it would take up time that I should devote to my "Oral History of Our Time," and I resolved then and there that I would never again accept regular employment unless I absolutely had to or starve but would cut my wants down to the bare bones and depend on friends and well-wishers to see me through. Since that fateful morning, the "Oral History" is the only thing that matters to me. I've been working on it for years, filling my fountain pen with free ink in the post office, writing in composition books, hundreds and thousands of composition books, millions of words by now, the longest literary project of all time, still of course unfinished and unpublished, but in process, seriously in process, in boxes of composition books held for me by literary friends all over the Village, all over New York. Homeless, I sleep in flophouses or doorways, don't wash or shave, get one haircut a year, scratch, wear clothes until my aroma finer than incense wrinkles the noses of those I approach at the parties and openings I go to for free food, and to meet people I can ask for a handout, a cigarette, people I can tell about my "Oral History," make them know that someday I will be known as a great genius.

He took my hand.
He would not let go.

Photograph of bearer

Augusta Savage

Passport image

The Rome Fellowship

1926

Doctor Du Bois fought for me. He arranged
a fellowship for me to go to Rome.
For a whole year. Fully paid for. Except
for the ocean liner to Italy.
The traditional bait and switch most Negroes live!
That's why our people had to invent the Blues!
How was I supposed to pay for the ticket?
I was still reeling when a hurricane
destroyed my family's house in West Palm Beach.
Mama and Papa, Irene, and my last-
born sisters and brother were left homeless.
They came to Harlem, to my one-bedroom.
The joyful family reunion. Papa's stroke.
The hospital. His paralysis. The bills.
Lord, you keep telling the ironic joke of Job.
The hours of sweating in a steam laundry
to make ends meet. Awake, surrounded by
the wall-to-wall breathing of those I love
the most in all the world, I almost laugh:
You made an artist a woman, and Black?

Gamin

1929

Art invents materials,
media, where there are none.
Poems written in matchbooks,
sculptures of papier-mâché.
Time to create art stolen
in miniature increments:
a few minutes here or there
to create one true gesture,
one movement toward truth.
My *Gamin*: spit and image
of my nephew Ellis, who
sleeps under the table and
has affected a hep strut
since he arrived in New York.

No longer a small-town boy,
he's wised up: he cocks his head,
pulls his cap's bill down
to one side, lifts his collar,
looks with a bemused, level
gaze at the ridiculous
and cruel stupidity
this world abounds in.
Fourteen going on forty,
his lips half-curved, knowingly,
Gamin turned my tide.

The *Crisis,*
the official magazine
of the NAACP, made
Gamin its cover.

And, like a falling line of
good-luck dominoes,
connected people saw it
and told people with money.
The Julius Rosenwald Fund
presented me with a check,
my family gave its blessing,
and now I'm in Montparnasse,
the left bank of the Seine, in
the 14th arrondissement.
I'm here studying sculpture
at the Académie de
la Grande Chaumière!
I'm in Paris (censored), France!

Gamin

SECTION II

1931-1940

Reclining Nude

Parlaying le Français

1929–1931

I speak not so good
le français. I am sculptor.
I seek dark model.

You sit down please here.
In Africa where you home?
Please remove the clothes.

Black woman can be
artist, sure. Please do not move.
How long you are here?

Monsieur Despiau,
please you say me of Rodin?
How he make that curve?

Thank you, gracious sirs,
for this very big honor.
Pain rewarded fades.

Dear Sister Zora,
Thank you for the fundraiser!
Every dollar helps!

Three years spent learning
technique, history, and French.
Au revoir, Paris!

Bonjour, Depression.
*L'art doit gagner du bacon!**
I'll open a school.

---

*Art's gotta bring home the bacon!

Studio

After Kerry James Marshall's painting of the same title, and remembering and imagining the Savage Studio of Arts & Crafts

In this space, quiet as a laboratory,
artists as focused as a team of chefs
in a five-star Michelin Guide restaurant
give themselves up to organized chaos.
They were born with a compulsion
deeper than skin-deep, deeper than Black:
Every cell of their bodies says *Make Art.*
Their hearts repeat: *Make Art, Make Art, Make Art.*

Here in the studio's silence,
artists demonstrate that freedom means
exploring unlimited potential,
playing a part in creation.
How beautiful the human body is.
How complex light is on Black skin.
How a story can emerge from colors.
How a yellow curve can become a dog.

Whether you're a woman, whether you're Black,
no matter who you are, you can make art.
Art rebuilds our hope for a shared future,
it restores our courage, revives our faith.
Here in the studio, as on cave walls,
our species reaches toward undying truths.
Every work of art was once unfinished:
part in the world, part imagined.

Bust of Aleksandr Pushkin

Hey, who, who has Negro blood isn't proud of
cousin Pushkin? Negroes who know who Pushkin was,
and those with no inkling of Russian history, we stand
straighter, knowing of the great-grandson of Hannibal—
an African page boy presented as a gift to the Sultan
of the Ottoman Empire, and then gifted again to Tsar
Peter the Great, then freed, educated, was a General,
a Governor, who married into a family of Russian
nobility and became father and grandfather of
brown Russian nobles, and great-grandfather
of the subject of my new bust, inspired by
an article in a Negro magazine about
"the greatest poet in Russian history,"
Aleksandr Sergeyevich Pushkin.
(But I've been calling him Sasha.)
I've built him from the pit of his
neck up to his crown, down to
his sternum, out to his wavy
curls, his muttonchop whiskers,
his close-razored, pride-lifted chin.
I've tooled smooth our immortal
poet's wide temples, his alertness,
his gracefully arched eyebrows,
high cheekbones, his handsome
nose. I've put his genius into his
large, gentle eyes. Dark genius
in his tender eyes. Our genius.
Our poet. On his shapely
mouth, faint vestiges of
our motherland,
our Ancestors.
Of Africa.
Of us.

Hot Pursuit

~~~~~~

1931

Joseph F. Gould, former president of the Race Pride League, who wrote
that riding in the same train car with a Negro may lead to his marrying your
sister; who wrote that America must keep the races apart so whites won't
object to equality; who wrote that the Jew and the Negro are physically and
temperamentally antipodes; who wrote that he wished "the literary world
were not quite as lousy with keik pants-pressers" as it is; who believes he is the
most brilliant historian of the twentieth century, that the history he is writing
of the world and his encounters with it will last as long as Homer, as long as
Shakespeare, as long as human language lasts, starts several letters a day.

My dear Mrs. Savage

My dear Miss Savage

My dear Augusta

Dear Augusta Savage

Dear Augusta

Dear Gussie

Dear Gus

Augusta

Gus

My dear Gussie

My darling Gus

My love, I've been calling and calling, many times a day, for so many weeks, and
sending you long daily letters you don't answer. Do you open them? Read them?
My Black darling, if you really believe in racial equity, you should want me
    as much as I want you. Oh, Baby, I'll marry you, I'll take care of you,

I'll learn to be Black for you, there must be
a drop of colored blood in my blue veins, enough to make you want me,
some way I can be Negro enough to win you, to hold your sweat-sleek
      Black body
in my arms, to touch my thin lips to your black skin, to taste
your Blackness, so come
to me, you sweet
morsel of filth,
come to me, come.

Head of Unidentified Youth

Leonore

1935

It wasn't easy
to sit still so long,
while Missus Savage
looked at me with narrowed eyes,
stepped close to gently push me
a teeny bit to one side,
or straightened the big red bow
Muh-Dear pinned to my sundress
to look like a butterfly
choosed my shoulder to rest on.
Or she moved my red hair bow
just a little bit
then stepped out of the
real world and back into "Art."
Art is what she says
she's making, and I'm helping.
Because Art's like when you say
a word with your mouth,
and then write it on paper.
Like the word "cat," and when you
come back the next day
or later, the word's still there,
but you can't quite remember
when your mouth said "cat"
or why. When the fidgets grew
inside me like a beehive,

I couldn't help it,
all them bees buzzing
louder and louder,
like Muh-Dear says the word "free"
use to buzz inside people
til they ranned away.
My bees ain't told me
to run away, even though
I heared the double-dutch ropes
slap on the sidewalk
and the big girls chant.
My bees buzzed louder, louder,
they said *Tell Missus Savage*
you got to wee-wee!

Leonore

Boy with Rabbit

1938

Long   ears
are, of   course,
the trade-   mark
of our   brother
Brer rabbit.   Like him,
we leap at   sudden noise,
flight our first,   perhaps best,
defense. A   slender Black
boy, naked,   shining wet after
a bath in the   summer outdoor
tub. Mama-   scrubbed, even
his ears clean,   a boy holds out
to a tentative   bunny a breath-
held moment   of almost touch.
Mamas know   of instants seized
by their ears,   of boys jerked up
in mid delight;   we know of drive-
by destinies. And   we know we may

all be the unnamed, uncountable toy soldiers of
future history. A Black boy, a bunny: the possibility
of trust, as before we were stolen, our innocence slain.
Generations later, we remember radical aloneness, the
bond of shared suffering. Besides the body's multitudinous
pain, we know inherited nightmares, both awake and asleep,
our DNA altered by experience, our vision uglified, our ability
to bless reversed. Ah, but first came the naked innocent, the
boy, as it were, in the garden, his willingness to share gladly
fruit that falls out of the generous tree just so a boy can pick
it up, nibble, and hold it out to the bunny's twitching nostrils.
Both are too young to know better. The tender arching nape,
the narrow shoulder, delicate hand, the unselfconscious belly
with its sweet rememory of life in the womb, and where sex
would proclaim gender, identity, a future beyond this flesh,
I allow this boy privacy: I will not look. I will let no one see.
I bestow erasure of what makes Black boys Black men,
and thus threatening. And thus dead. What makes Black
boys playing under streetlights hoodlums, carriers of
potential taint, seductive viral invaders of a purer
blood, I do not reveal. Let the clay model absence,
let each tiny pellet I press on save this boy forever
from the racist, comparative gaze. No one will see the
strength of his wire armature, but I know it's there, as it is
in each Black boy who is twisted, crushed, beaten down. My iron
support holds him secure as love now, plumb from jugular notch to
the inner left ankle, clay packed onto spine, thorax, pelvis, the relaxed
thigh and the load-bearing, the shoulder blades, the knees. The amazing
curves and planes of human anatomy. How can humans not recognize our
universal beauty? The external oblique muscles, great latissimus, sartorius,
the spiraling formations, the rhythm of the human shape. And there, an arch
reaching on hind legs to the edge of trust, a bunny trembles, drunk with hope.

51

Harlem Community Art Center

※

Savage directed her (renamed) school while working as a WPA administrator, 1937–1939

The Negro Mecca.
The hub of Negro culture.
Paris Noir. But so reduced.

The stock market crash
made rich white people
jump out of windows.

The Great Depression
wore big walking-around holes
in the shoe soles of Black folk.

But making art feeds hungers.
Those who create live
in so many other ways.

Thank God for the Depression,
parent of the WPA.
For government-supported art.

WPA projects
present the faces
who make up America.

My work has become
the works of all my students.
They may be my legacy.

I see it this way:
Once I played a violin;
now I'm waving a baton.

Harlem Community Art Center

The Harp

1938

The Harp

face   face   face   face   face   face   face   face   face   face   face   face
Suddenly I stand bareheaded in a shower of opportunities! No: surrounded by a cloud
of migrating butterflies! Unbelievably blessed! My students' successes made me proud,
but this commission, this pinnacle, humbles me to joyful tears! I'm asked to create
a sculpture for next year's World's Fair! After the bitterness, this shock of sweet.
I'll have to make something truly monumental. A grand statue will convey
a strong truth no one can curse at, call names, or shove out of the way.
I want to speak the Black-people-all-Sunday-morning truth of a choir.
Out of their glad hearts, full throats, wide mouths, their voices soar
over weariness like a twilight sky full of swallows skimming a lake.
I'll take time away from my work to work full-time on my work.
Black children. Black children singing. Triumphant hope?

Could I sculpt black love triumphant as a black harp?   HIS HAND

How? Twelve strings? And each harp string a child?
Each child individual, a recognizable singing self.
What would they be singing? A gospel hymn?
How about the Negro National Anthem?
Millions will see my piece next year.
  They can see, if they can't hear,
   the words Black people sing
   when we are celebrating
boy   being together again, having
    survived. Lift every voice and sing,
words we sing, making earth and heaven ring
   with the triumphant hope of mere being.

Augusta Savage with two of her statuettes

Opening of the Salon of Contemporary Negro Arts

June 7, 1939

It's my gallery's big night.
Rented *flûtes* of chilled *champagne*,
Hors d'oeuvres passed on silver trays.
And look at the crowd:
Negro men in tuxedos,
brownskin ladies in silk gowns,
clink and chatter, perfumed air.
Like Paris, with more color.
Harlem's artistic vanguard,
and white people with checkbooks.
This is America's first
Negro-owned, curated, and
exhibiting gallery.
It will be an art Mecca!
Here is Harlem's self-portrait!

(Ooh, girl, she think she something.
Act like she's a damn genius,
all cultured and all.)

(It was rather close.
And there must have been
ten Negroes to each of us.
We don't have to go back. Let's
send a little donation.)

57

Realization

Three-quarter size. Full size would break the heart.
She, still bare-breasted from the auction block,
sits staring, perhaps realizing what
will happen to them next. There is no child,
though there must be a child who will be left
behind, or who was auctioned separately.
Her arms are limp, defeated, her thin hands
lie still in surrender.
He cowers at her side,
his head under her arm,
his body pressed to hers
like a boy hiding behind his mother.
He should protect his woman. He is strong,
his shoulder and arm muscled from hard work,
his hand, thickened by labor, on her thigh
as if to comfort, though he can't protect.
His brow is furrowed, his eyes blank, unfocused.
What words are there to describe hopelessness?
A word that means both bull-whipped and spat on?
Is there a name for mute, depthless abyss?
A word that means Where the hell are you, God?
What would they ask God, if they could believe?
But how can they believe, while the blue sky
smiles innocently, pretends nothing is wrong.
They stood stripped up there, as they were described
like animals who couldn't understand

how cheap a life can be made.
Their naked feet. Her collarbone. The vein
traveling his bicep. Gussie's answer
to presidents on Mount Rushmore,
to monumental generals whose stars
and sabers say Black pain
did not then and still does not matter.

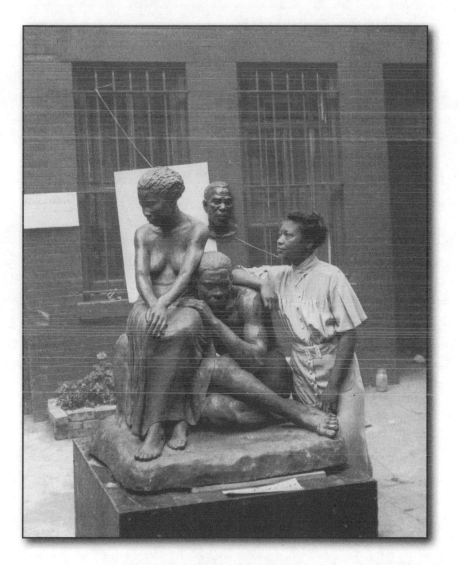

Realization

Bust of James Weldon Johnson

1939

Many biographies reside in every bust.
But in this one the memories arise and push each
other aside as I work. Years ago I hoped to sculpt the
face emerging on this modeling stand. As I adjust the
turntable, I see again the horizon-seeker I met back in our
Florida days. Since then I've read about, or read, or even
occasionally run into Mr. Johnson in Harlem over the years,
watched him emerge, from school principal and lawyer to
poet, diplomat, novelist, editor of Negro anthologies,
a Broadway lyricist, the executive secretary of the NAACP.
Now the familiar anatomy of his shapely cranium has been
measured by my calipers, from ear to ear, nose tip to chin,
from the end of his broad mustache to the outer corner of
his eye. Each pinch of clay I lay on builds up the individual
features that comprised his distinguished bearing. With
what grace he bore the mantle of his gift. He must have known
from boyhood that there was something out there waiting for
him to take shape from his heritage of freedom won, education
achieved, and culture loved; that he would bear the sense
of Black responsibility, which drives the Black artist to make
art matter. His eyes were intense, steel gray, inward-looking.
They made me feel seen. To create a good bust
you have to know your subject, then mash on, with the warm clay,
the ways of living and thinking that make up character.
Working, I hum lightly the anthem he wrote for us:
Lift every voice and sing, till earth and heaven ring,

ring with the harmonies of Liberty . . .
His words, the inspiration for my strongest work.
How I wish I were sculpting from life, and not
from photographs and memory. He seemed
to be driven to lead us upward, to create wise beauty,
to do as much as he could toward a better future
before his car stalled on the tracks last year as the train came.

Bust of James Weldon Johnson

Head of John Henry

1940

How to suggest nappy hair
without forming every curl?
The forehead so much
easier: high, broad,
smooth, it reflects light.
Eyebrow to eyebrow,
large-irised eye to dark eye,
nestle over the cheekbones.
Someone might catch, from the tip
of John Henry's straight-bridged nose,
a glimpse into his future.
Wide, symmetrical nostrils,
full lips, shapely cupid's bow,
a square jawline, a firm chin,
head held proudly high:
John Henry stands on the brink
of Negro manhood,
when a boy's beautiful life
becomes endangered.

Up Down Up

1940

The Harp was the most
popular, most photographed
artwork at the Fair!

Copies and postcards
of *The Harp* were what tourists
took home from New York!

A spotlit feature
in (censored) *LIFE* magazine!
A (white) gallery!

I couldn't afford
to have *The Harp* cast in bronze,
so it was destroyed.

My assistant, who
replaced me during my leave,
won't give up my job.

My board sides with her.
What is fame, without funding?
All my ventures fail.

My former students
are moving the ball forward:
art beyond my dreams!

Romare Bearden!
Gwendolyn Knight! Jake Lawrence!
Ernie Crichlow! Selma Burke!

The (white) gallery
shipped my pieces to be shown
in another state!

My shipped-off pieces
have apparently been lost.
They were uninsured.

Sculptors! Painters! Print-
makers! Muralists!
Art teachers! Seers! Dreamers!

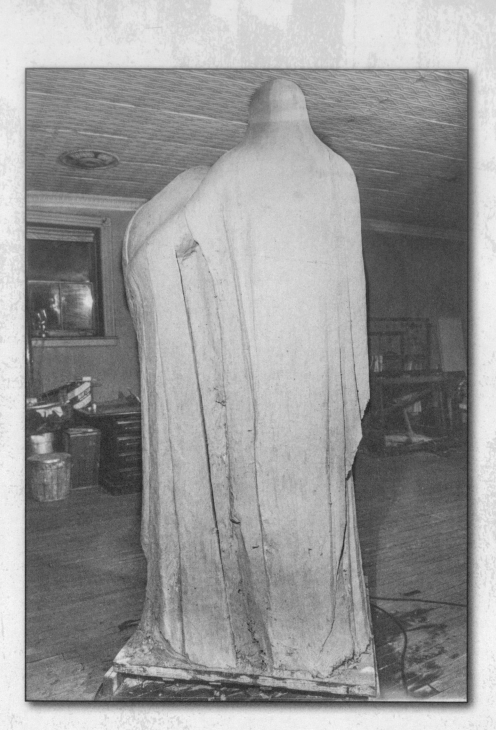

After the Glory

After the Glory

Unfinished, 1939

So, shall I cut my losses and move on?
Have I been barking my head off up the wrong tree?
Does a monument carved in marble drapery
show stubborn adherence to white traditions that are long gone?

Fame, glory: a bacon fat fire in a frying pan.
Bravo! Presto chango! Voici voilà! And it's out.
Days later, people wonder what all the shouting was about.
Am I one of the chosen, or an also-ran?

Have I contributed something positive to the human race?
The questions haunt me, haunt every artist called
to partake in creation, to bring artistry into the world.
Does my work make the world a better place?

Maybe I should just retire to a lake isle
where I can be freer than I was as a child.

Salon

I once wondered where
it comes from, this hunger
to pull something out of yourself,
like the spider spinning the thread that
leads through time's labyrinthine corridors.
But then the ache became as much myself as
the syllables "Augusta Christine Fells Savage." Me.
And my thread keeps following me, telling my history,
leaving a trail perhaps someone will someday follow.
It others me and defines my otherness. It's the one word
my lips and my tongue desire to speak and can't. It longs
beyond touch, exhaled in every breath, like the secret tears
of a child waking from a flying dream to want. Art. Why is the
artist made to be an artist? Why does the gene pool keep on
creating would-be creators, making more to labor tirelessly?
Most of our work is so soon forgotten. We still hunger, reach
for the beyond. So I hold kitchen table *salons* where my
beautiful Black young student artists break cornbread
together, lift a glass with my family, and laugh.
This is where we are and who we are, in this
splendid moment, hosting thoughts
we hope will wake up peace.

The Harp at the World's Fair

SECTION III

1941-1962

The Pugilist

※

1942

Like a kid in a playground fight
being beaten up by bullies
(guess whose skin is dark,
whose tends toward summer
freckles or sunburn, and who's
pissed off because whose ancestors
kidnapped whose ancestors,
thereby changing the population of two
continents with rape and intentional
extermination),
the man-child holds
his head high,
his arms folded
across his chest. He
refuses to surrender.
Yes, he stares right back
at a red face with hard fists,
a red face with an ugly mouth,
a red face with screaming eyes,
a red face in the surging mob,
a red face under a red cap,
a red face under swirling lights,
and like a kid on the playground
he looks straight back
into the red face.
Unbowed, defiant, tight-jawed,

he looks straight back.
Even though
one of his eyes
leaks a tear.

The Pugilist

The Return of the Genius Author of What Will Undoubtedly Be the Longest and Most Beautifully Written Unpublished Book in the History of the World

1943

They've let him out of the hospital.
But he's still out of his (censored) mind.
The telephone's ringing off the hook.
Thick, scribbled letters come every day.
They make no sense, and make me tremble.
He knows where I work, and he could look
up my home address in the phone book.
The white literati think Joe Gould
is a (censored) genius. But I know
the licked-lips smile, the rump pat, the smell.
Add together his delusions of grandeur
his narcissism, racism, lice.
What happens when a Black woman screams?
When I pick up the phone, he speaks gull.

Augusta Savage presenting model to Grover Whalen

Minerva

Head of Minerva

1945

Goddess of war and art, you've got a lot
to answer for: from mustard gas to the Bomb,
and what's between. Just think of the lives
and the works of art that have been sacrificed
on altars dedicated to false gods,
in this century still less than half gone.
What more will you let history perpetrate
in these paroxysms of white hate?

That's right: Lower your head, shake it slowly
in resignation, disbelief, in shame.
Yet, working by the light you emanate,
my hands have found the brilliance of the clay.
We lose ourselves in war. Art meets our gaze
and gives us back ourselves, with our lives changed.

No Forwarding Address

Saugerties, NY, 1945–1961

Miss Savage doesn't live here anymore.
I don't know exactly where she is,
but I hear tell she stays up in the Catskills,
in the moneyed boondocks, nowadays.

Maybe somebody she met in the art world
gave her a hand up, helped her find a place.
I heard her daughter may have some friends up there.
Well, bless her heart. We all deserve some peace.

The grapevine says she's got a chicken-coop-
turned-artist's-studio behind her house,
that she raises squabs for fancy restaurants
and takes care of laboratory mice.
That she hears the Hudson. That it's a white world.
She takes the bus back every other week, for a press and curl.

Augusta Savage's home in Saugerties, New York

Laughing Boy

Bust of Steven "Barry" Baran

1951

I didn't know I was running until I stopped.
I planted flowers, started growing food.
Got a dog, Myra. Take her for long walks
through woods and fields, and on our unpaved road.

Picked out a favorite place from which to watch
the Hudson's perpetual motion flow—
like moments born, then borne into the past.
I couldn't have dreamed this life, sixty years ago.

My neighbors invite me into their homes.
The passing Greyhound driver beeps and waves.
I didn't know I was capable of such calm,
such privileged distance from the nation's news.
My new friends Jean and Steve will laugh with joy
when they see this Christmas bust of their scalawag boy.

Chicken-Foot Soup

Raising chickens for restaurants, you eat what's left.
The neighbor children who hang out at Miss Savage's house
will remember blackberry picking, fishing in the creek, collecting
puffball mushrooms, roasting potatoes and ears of corn
in open bonfires, gathering garden flowers, tending pigeons,
feeding chickens, pumping water in the kitchen, lighting kerosene lamps,
listening with open mouths to Miss Savage's wonderful stories,
and inventing polite ways to say no thanks to Miss Savage's most
frequently proffered lunch: Chicken-Foot Soup.

½ teaspoon oil

a few sprigs of fresh thyme

4 cloves garlic, minced

1 small onion, finely chopped

8 chicken feet, toe tips and claws cut off

4 chicken necks

10 cups water

1 small potato, peeled and cut into chunks

2 or 3 carrots, peeled and chopped

2 stalks celery, chopped

1 ½ cups pumpkin, cut in two-inch chunks

1 hot pepper

pinch of black pepper

2 or 3 ears fresh corn on the cob, if in season, cut in pieces

1 teaspoon salt

Instructions:

Place oil in a large pot. When oil is hot, sauté thyme, garlic, and onion for a couple of minutes. Add chicken and cook, stirring, for a few minutes. Add water and bring to a boil. Cover and keep on slow boil for about 45 minutes. Add potato, carrots, celery, pumpkin, and hot pepper and black pepper. Cover and let simmer for about 20 minutes, or until vegetables are soft. If you have fresh corn, add it last. Serve with or without chicken necks and feet.

Miss Savage serves it without necks, with feet.
Thank you, I'm not hungry, Miss Savage, the children lie.

Girl with Braids

1951

What's brewing under that crown of braids,
Sweetheart, as you sit still as a mouse?
How many clock ticks have you counted
as I've replicated your eyebrows
with my wire tools? I like your father,
the nice Pastor, and the generous,
careful welcome his church has offered.
How he blushed and stammered that day you
lilted, "Miss Savage, are you a maid?"
Shocked, he asked where that idea came from.
You shrugged with wide eyes, lifting your palms.
A tide of tears came in, overflowed.

I waved away his apology:
It's in our air, the light we see by.

Final Commission

~~~~~~

Bust of Poultney Bigelow, 1951

He's frail, so I have to go to him, driving the rattletrap Pontiac my
benefactor/friend Mr. Knaust gave me so I could drive myself to my job
caring for lab mice in his little cancer research facility. Knowing who I used
to be, Mr. Knaust arranged the commission, the transfer of funds that are
enough to get me through next year (if I'm thrifty, maybe even longer than
that), to create a bust of Mister Poultney Bigelow, one of the mansioned,
society-page, pinky-lifting, highbrow, Ivy League Hudson Valley neighbors
I will never in a million years hobnob with, or even encounter in a grocery
store line. THE Poultney Bigelow, Mr. Knaust exclaimed, as if I must
certainly have heard the name before. I bet the kids he went to school with
called him Poultry.

I park beside the (huge) house.
Beyond its brick magnificence
the Hudson passes
without making history.
I'm ushered up carpeted stairs
with a curved mahogany banister,
past several not-half-bad oil portraits,
to a small, beautiful sitting room.
And here sits this thin, long-limbed
old man, well over ninety,
with . . . depthless eyes . . .
a fluffy white mustache and beard,
a full head of white wavy hair,

white eyebrows, and

. . . depthless eyes . . .

I've been told he comes from what

I understand is a very distinguished

family, something about Kaiser Wilhelm,

Mark Twain, an ambassador,

about the *New York Post*.

Maybe they owned it? Where did

France come in? Horizontals crease

his forehead, deep verticals

divide the brows, a long, narrow head,

large, low-slung ears. An unbowed armature.

He smiles expectantly.

Small wrinkles at the corners of

. . . depthless eyes . . . He asks

if I will, I say yes,

we can start next week.

But can I make a true portrait,

knowing so little of who he is?

Can I capture ninety invisible years?

Ninety wealthy, brilliant, cultured, well-bred,

Yale-educated, tall white man years?

I have no idea

what his eyes have seen,

what lies there, submerged.

I get up, shake his bony,

paper-skinned hand, and leave.

As I turn old Betsy's key

I know I've made a terrible mistake.

I haven't read

a single word of his books.

Poultney Bigelow

Juneteenth Barbecue

Bust of Genevieve Nelson, 1953

The bus from Saugerties to Manhattan
stops only a short walk from my new front porch.
In four hours I can be waiting my turn
in Hattie's chair in Clarissa's beauty shop.
In four hours I can be surrounded by
delicious Harlem gossip, by laughter
that takes me to those bid whist tournaments
back in the Twenties, when we lived on hope.
From one world to another, white to Black:
Myra, a few friends, quiet, seclusion,
to what I believed then was important,
that turned out to be the illusion
ambition creates, of a legacy
which will survive infirmity and death.

I had my little youth, and I got old.
I had my little fame, and the world changed.

The bus delivers friends and family
to my annual Juneteenth barbecue.
Come rain or shine, my Saugerties retreat
will be full of Negroes for one weekend
of honest-to-God, running-wild freedom.
Children and grandchildren, mosquito bites,
hot dogs, potato salad, marshmallows,
hand-cranked ice cream, histories, and the stars.

Beds, sofas, and floors covered with sleepers.
After Sunday breakfast we wave goodbye,
and Myra and I take a little nap.
Then I uncover what I'm working on:
a bust of my neighbor: Lois Kimble,
who sometimes stops by with a plate of scones.

I had my little youth, and I got old.
I had my little fame, and the world changed.

Genevieve Nelson

I Don't Know

1959

Penguin

Irene and
her husband and
stepchildren drove up
last weekend, with the new Fats Domino,
a loaf of rye, some sliced pastrami, and
the latest hearsay about now
medium-famous Harlem artist
friends: who's exhibiting, whose
books have been well reviewed. They
might have driven from Mars, that's how
far I am from needing, as for years I did, to
make a name that will survive me. Irene set
the kids to work gathering the last tomatoes.
Her husband, a good man, he works two jobs
and drove the whole way, lay cloud-gazing in
the hammock. I wish Mama and I could have
talked the way Irene and I can, intimate as sister-
friends. I'm thankful for her forgiveness, for the
loving upbringing my family gave her. Thank God
Irene doesn't feel that unrelievable itch that drove
me to turn my natural-born life inside out pursuing . . .
Pursuing what? Ah, well. She said she's glad I have
electricity now, and indoor plumbing, and that my
telephone will help us keep in touch. And she says it
reduces her anxiety about my living all the   way up
in the hinterlands, and alone. Yet and still, she   added,
you're still dependent on the kindness of (nice,   but)
white people, at the age when you should be able   to
take yourself, with your aches and pains, your gone
joints, your grunts and groans, someplace where we
who love you can take care of you, Mama. Yes, yes, I
said. But I feel I should make art, for the simple joy of it,
for pleasure. No ego, no ambition, art with one goal: I don't
know: happiness? I'd like to make free art, for once. Even
though kneading clay makes me pant, and moan with an
aching back, I know what I'm on earth to do. But I'm tired of
carrying Truth around like a marble block. I'm sick of meaning. I want
to have fun while I can. To play. To create free sculptures that make people
smile, leave 'em laughing. Sculptures of what?   I don't know: penguins?

Crows

What if to taste and see, to notice things,
to stand each *is* up against emptiness
for a moment or an eternity—
images collected in consciousness
like a tree alone on the horizon—
is the main reason we're on this planet?
The *food's here* of the first crow to arrive,
numbers two and three at a safe distance,
then approaching the hand-created taste
of leftover coconut macaroons.
The instant sparks in the earth's awareness.

Bird Feeder

Live not for battles won.
Live not for the-end-of-the-song.
Live in the along.

GWENDOLYN BROOKS

Approaching seventy, I've learned to live,
at last. I realize that I have not
accomplished half of what I've struggled for,
that I surrendered too many battles
and seldom celebrated those I won.
Approaching seventy, I'm learning to live
without ambition: a calm lake face, not
a train bound for success and glory. For
the first time, I've relaxed my hands on the
controls, leaned back to watch the coming end.
Asked, I'd tell you my life is made out of
the things I didn't do as much as the
things I did do. Did I sing a love song?
Approaching seventy, I've learned to live
without wanting much more than the light in
the catbird window seat, where, watching the
voracious fist-sized tweets, I hum along.

Awake

Suddenly I woke in the midst of life,
aware suddenly of the misseds of life,
who disappeared into the mists of life.

A Gift to Be

Every millisecond pleads
as I near the age my mother reached.
In every plea a seed of thanks,
from this speck of consciousness
collecting memories, this mote
of cosmic experience.
Are we welcomed back,
or are we raindrops in a sea?
What a gift to be. To wonder.

Bas Relief of a Female Dancer

1959

My work in an old cookie sheet
on the crowded kitchen table.
Salt and pepper shakers, sugar
bowl, and a cup of darjeeling tea
left to grow cold. The morning sun
crowing like a giant rooster.
Rolling pin aside and my tools
within easy reach. I have to
look down my nose through bifocals
at the young dancer emerging
from an invisible background.
Caught in the middle of a step,
her contours carved and added on,
arms lifted and torso twisted,
she twirls out of adolescence
into self-authenticity,
as the clock on the wall tick-tocks.

As if hearing African drums
or summoning Terpsichore,
imagination makes the dance
with disappearing brown fingers.
The artist must stand face-to-face
with sadness, suffering, and death.
Loss is the wisdom behind song.
Art can't dance without *duende*.

I lean in, focus on her curls.
The dancer gazes back at me
out of black Mona Lisa eyes.

Bas Relief of a Female Dancer

I have created nothing really beautiful, really lasting, but if I can inspire one of these youngsters to develop the talent I know they possess, then my monument will be in their work.

—AUGUSTA SAVAGE

AFTERWORD
by Tammi Lawson

The world into which Augusta Christine Fells was born on February 29, 1892, in Green Cove Springs, Florida, offered few opportunities to Black Americans. A leap-year baby, she was the seventh of fourteen children born to Cornelia and Edward Fells, both of whom had been born into the harsh system of American slavery. While the Thirteenth Amendment, ratified in 1865, abolished slavery, it did not end the racial oppression Black people faced. Her father earned a living as a carpenter, fisherman, and preacher affiliated with the African Methodist Episcopal Church (AME), a denomination founded in response to discrimination against Black people in white churches. Despite the realities and limitations of her time, Augusta Savage forged a life through art and creativity.

Augusta was a precocious child who quickly advanced from making mud pies to shaping clay figurines of the animals she saw around her. Her father, misunderstanding the second of the Ten Commandments, which forbids the worship of "graven images," felt that what she created was sinful. He beat her if he caught her making them, or if he discovered any of her trove of sculptures. Augusta later recalled that her father "almost whipped all the art out of me."

Perhaps to get away from her strict parents, when she was fifteen (1907), Augusta married John T. Moore and gave birth to her only child, Irene. Her husband died after a brief illness. The widowed child bride and mother returned to her parents' home. Back in high school, Augusta began to receive recognition for her artistic talent. The principal offered her a part-time job teaching clay modeling, with a salary of one dollar a day.

Augusta moved with her extended family to West Palm Beach, where she worked at various jobs and enrolled briefly in one of the nearby HBCUs (Historically Black Colleges and Universities), possibly the school for girls founded in 1904 by Mary McLeod Bethune. Augusta briefly attended Tallahassee State

University (now known as Florida A&M). In 1915, Augusta married James Savage. Their union soon ended in divorce, but she kept his name for the rest of her life.

In 1919, Augusta exhibited her sculptures at the West Palm Beach County Fair, selling most of her work and winning twenty-five dollars and a blue ribbon. Impressed by her exhibition at the fair, the fair's superintendent, George Graham Currie, became one of her patrons and commissioned her to sculpt a portrait bust of himself. He also encouraged her to move to New York City to pursue her dream of studying art.

Encouraged by her success and probably discouraged by the epidemic of lynchings that engulfed the South at the end of World War I, when Black soldiers returned home from Europe wearing military uniforms and displaying newfound self-respect, Augusta joined what became known as the Great Migration, when millions of Black people left the southern United States to escape the racist segregation and political disenfranchisement commonly known as Jim Crow.

Leaving Florida and all that she knew—including her young daughter, Irene, who stayed with grandparents, aunts, uncles, and cousins—in search of a chance for a better life, Augusta arrived in New York City in 1921 with less than five dollars, a portfolio, and a reference letter written by the superintendent of the West Palm Beach County Fair. The letter was also an introduction to Solon Borglum, a noted American sculptor and member of the American Academy of Fine Arts, who had an art school in the city. However impressed he may have been with Augusta, Borglum realized she could not pay for classes. He referred her to his friend Kate L. Reynolds at the Cooper Union for the Advancement of Science and Art, a merit-based college in downtown New York, which was tuition-free at the time. Taken with Augusta's talent, Reynolds immediately accepted her into the School of Art. Living in Harlem, Augusta found employment as a domestic and laundress. Driven to excel, she advanced quickly through undergraduate work, finishing the program in three years instead of four.

In Harlem, Augusta fit right in. After all, she held a degree in fine art and she was surrounded by other talented Black artists. In the 1920s, Harlem was a cultural mecca. Its flourishing creative community was the nexus of young writers such as Langston Hughes, Claude McKay, and Zora Neale Hurston. Duke Ellington played nightly at the Cotton Club. Fellow Floridian James Weldon Johnson, the noted author, lawyer, diplomat, and composer, lived there. Philosopher Alain

Locke, one of the progenitors of what was to become known as the "New Negro Movement," and Charles S. Johnson, sociologist, writer, educator, and director of research and investigation at the Chicago Urban League, lived there as well. Augusta had arrived in Harlem at the beginning of what we now call the Harlem Renaissance.

Supporting all creative endeavors was the Division of Negro Literature, History and Prints, at the New York Public Library 135th Street Branch, which was later renamed the Schomburg Center for Research in Black Culture. Augusta spent so much time there studying books about European and African art that the librarians took notice. She was commissioned by the library to sculpt a bust of the eminent historian and sociologist W. E. B. Du Bois, cofounder of the NAACP (National Association for the Advancement of Colored People), and editor of its magazine, *The Crisis*. Du Bois, a highly influential public intellectual, viewed artists as an essential part of the true representation of Black people and Black culture.

In 1923, Augusta was awarded a scholarship to study sculpture at the Fontainebleau School of Fine Arts in France. She felt vindicated for pursuing her dream and was eager to continue her studies in Europe, having been accepted by the French selection committee, which was made up of French artists. But, upon learning that Augusta was Black, the American selection committee rescinded the award. Devastated but determined, Augusta took her case to the public with an intense letter-writing campaign to shed light on her situation and to advocate for fair and unbiased treatment for future Black applicants. Her case was covered in both Black and white newspapers across the country. The one dissenting member of the committee, Hermon MacNeil, president of the National Sculpture Society, invited her to study privately with him in his studio in Long Island, New York.

In addition to this professional setback, Augusta underwent incredible personal adversity. Shortly after, her father was paralyzed by a stroke, and a hurricane destroyed the family home, forcing her to move most of the family north to live with her, all supported by her meager income. At one point, there were nine people living in Augusta's one-bedroom apartment. Her father and one of her brothers died in the space of a year.

W. E. B. Du Bois recommended her for a scholarship to study in Rome, but she had spent her savings taking care of her family and could not afford to go.

Disappointed, angry, and galvanized to action, she was drawn to the Universal Negro Improvement Association (UNIA), founded by Marcus Garvey (whose bust she had sculpted), an organization dedicated to uplifting people of African ancestry. There she found love again, and in 1923 she married Robert L. Poston, a journalist and newspaper publisher, who was secretary general, the second-in-command of the organization. Shortly after the wedding, Poston sailed on a mission to Africa to secure land for a mass emigration of African Americans to Liberia. The mission ultimately struggled to secure adequate funding, and Poston left Liberia deeply disappointed. During his return home, he fell ill with pneumonia and died. Devastated and pregnant with their child, Augusta went into premature labor. Their daughter, Roberta, lived for only a few days.

Despite—or perhaps because of—these unimaginable hardships, Augusta was driven to make art. She mounted exhibits of her work and that of other African American artists in New York libraries, social clubs, and with the Harmon Foundation, gaining favorable reviews and continued support from those institutions. In 1929, she created a sculpture of her young nephew, Ellis Ford, celebrating his undeniably African American physiognomy. Entitled *Gamin*, meaning "street urchin," the bust featured a boy with his cap tilted to the side, a mischievous expression on his face. After six long years of unrelenting work and incredible misfortune, Augusta finally gained recognition for *Gamin*. It was featured on the cover of the NAACP's magazine, *The Crisis*. She was awarded a Julius Rosenwald fellowship to study abroad, and a Carnegie Foundation award that allowed her to extend her study for two extra years. She went to Paris at last.

For centuries, artists from around the world went to Paris, the City of Light, to be educated and inspired by its resources and galleries. In Paris, Augusta studied at the Académie de la Grande Chaumière and exhibited her work at the Société des Artistes Français de Beaux-Arts and at the Grand Palais. She won high praise and honorable mentions at the Salons d'Automne and de Printemps. She also sent work to be included in the Harmon Foundation exhibitions at the 135th Street branch library, growing her reputation in New York at the same time. While she was in Europe, the stock market crash plunged the United States into the Great Depression. Bankruptcy and poverty descended on the nation, and art became a luxury.

Upon her triumphant return to Harlem in 1932, Augusta was reunited with her daughter Irene, who was then a young woman of twenty-four, and the rest of her family. Her professional life also continued to flourish. In 1934, she was elected to the National Association of Women Painters and Sculptors (later renamed the National Association of Women Artists), becoming its first African American member. Her work received national exposure, exhibited at the Anderson Galleries' tenth annual exhibition of the Salons of America. Her sculpture *Realization*, exhibited at the Architectural League, earned an honorable mention. But recognition does not necessarily feed hungry mouths.

Augusta began to establish herself as an influential teacher. She first offered art classes at the 135th Street branch library, but quickly outgrew that space and opened the Savage Studio of Arts and Crafts in a larger space on West 143rd Street. Her students included Jacob Lawrence, William Artis, Norman Lewis, Morgan and Marvin Smith, and Ernest Crichlow, who went on to become some of the most important American artists of the twentieth century. Augusta was commissioned to create busts of luminous African Americans such as James Weldon Johnson and Frederick Douglass, as well as of everyday people in the community such as Genevieve Nelson, a registered nurse employed at Harlem Hospital.

In 1933, Franklin D. Roosevelt signed into legislation the Federal Emergency Relief Act, and in 1935 he created the Works Progress Administration (WPA), later the Work Projects Administration. The purpose of the WPA was to create all kinds of jobs at every skill level to preserve professional and technical skills while helping individuals maintain their self-respect. This legislation put hundreds of thousands of people, including artists, to work across the United States—the first time in our country's history that artists could be paid by the government to work full-time in their craft. To ensure that her students were being given an opportunity to direct projects and teach within the WPA program, Augusta established in 1935 the Harlem Artists Guild, with artist Charles Alston as co-director and Norman Lewis as treasurer. They came together to address the concerns of Black artists and fight for jobs and assignments in the federal art projects in New York City. With money from the WPA, she was able to expand and offer classes in painting, drawing, costume design, composition, sculpture, ceramics, metalcraft, weaving, rug making, lithography, block printing, and photography. She opened the Harlem Art Workshop, which outgrew its original space and moved to a town house at 306 West 141st Street. "306" became a think tank where noted African American writers and artists gathered to discuss issues and concerns affecting Black communities. Among those contributing to these robust discussions were writers Richard Wright, Ralph Ellison, and Countee Cullen.

Conveying to her students the art techniques she had learned while studying in Europe, Augusta encouraged them to create artwork reflective of Harlem culture and African American identity. She successfully mounted an exhibition of their work at the Harlem YMCA. She became assistant supervisor of the WPA classes held at the Uptown Art Laboratory and employed former students as teachers. Three years later, with the financial support of the WPA/Federal Art Project (FAP), Augusta opened the Harlem Community Art Center on 125th Street. Providing instruction to 1,500 students and employing a cadre of artists, the center, recognized for excellence, became the model for WPA-sponsored art schools across the nation and drew influential visitors such as First Lady Eleanor Roosevelt.

By the late 1930s, Augusta Savage's name was synonymous with hard work and success. In 1937, the Board of Design commissioned thirty-five sculptures to decorate the architecture, garden, and plaza in the "World of Tomorrow" section of the 1939 World's Fair, to be held at Flushing Meadows–Corona Park in Queens, New York. One of the thirty-five sculptors commissioned was Augusta Savage. She took for her theme "Lift Every Voice and Sing." The idea of the fair was to promote optimism and to look to the future. They made the progressive choice to celebrate the unique contributions made by African Americans to music, and to oppose segregation of artwork by racial groups.

Augusta discussed her ideas about her commission with colleagues at her art school, according to George Murray, her business manager and the model for the front piece holding the scroll for "Lift Every Voice and Sing." For Augusta, this was an opportunity to honor her recently deceased friend and fellow Floridian, civil-rights activist, writer, and composer James Weldon Johnson. In her presentation notes to the design board, Augusta explained her design: "I have taken for my theme the national Negro anthem. It is a poem written by the late James Weldon Johnson, and set to the music by his brother, Rosamond Johnson. The title is 'Lift Every Voice and Sing,' known as the Negro National Anthem." Knowing this would be her first monumental work, Augusta applied for a one-year leave of absence from her job as Director of the Harlem Community Art Center, in order to devote herself full-time to the World's Fair commission.

By this time, Augusta clearly was one of the most influential artists in Harlem. She had graduated from a prestigious university, won fellowships that funded her art studies in Europe, exhibited on two continents, established art schools, and curated exhibitions. She had flexed her political muscle by organizing a successful campaign and organization to obtain administrative and teaching positions for her students. Her apartment had become known as a gathering place for artists, an informal salon for discussions of art and politics, and for rollicking games of the card game called bid whist.

In 1939, the year of the World's Fair, she took a hugely ambitious giant step and opened the first ever Black-owned and -operated commercial art gallery in America, the Salon of Contemporary Negro Art. It represented established African American artists including Richmond Barthé, Lois Mailou Jones, Meta Vaux Warrick Fuller, and Beauford Delaney. The grand opening of the Salon, reminiscent of gallery openings she had attended in Paris, was a formal affair with gowns and tuxedos, hors d'oeuvres, and champagne served in stemware. In order to succeed, an art gallery needs not only artists and their art but also art collectors, people willing and able to invest money in art. America was still struggling to come out of the Depression. African Americans did not inherit a tradition of being collectors of expensive fine art. The Salon of Contemporary Negro Art was short-lived and a major disappointment. But Augusta had done it; she'd made a dream of hers briefly come true.

Augusta's World's Fair piece, called *The Harp*, was a sixteen-foot-tall plaster sculpture painted to look like black basalt. It took the form of a huge harp made of African American figures of various heights representing the strings. It was placed in the courtyard of the Contemporary Arts Pavilion at the World's Fair and was seen by millions of visitors. Maquettes of the crowd-pleasing work were made and sold as very popular souvenirs of the fair. Augusta's participation in the fair and the popularity of *The Harp* should have buoyed her artistic career. But after the installation, when she returned to work as director of the Harlem Community Art Center, artist Gwendolyn Bennett, who had been her temporary replacement, refused to leave. To make matters worse, the governing board of the Community Art Center sided with Bennett. Augusta Savage was out of a job. And then, at the end of the fair, she was unable to raise the funds to have *The Harp* moved, stored, or cast in bronze. Although Fisk University and an insurance company in Florida expressed interest in purchasing the sculpture, neither secured funding by the time the fair was over. Her monumental plaster sculpture, her masterpiece, was destroyed.

There are many speculations as to why Augusta Savage's career seemingly ended. One possible factor may have been the discouragement of feeling "passed over," as the art world moved away from her classic style and increasingly toward abstraction. Some of her work was lost in transit to a gallery show in another state. It is possible that she destroyed much of her remaining work. She was rumored to have been harassed by Joe Gould, a white writer reputed to be a genius and clearly a madman. There was the onset of World War II. Augusta was almost fifty, still piecing together a living. It is not hard to imagine that she must have felt defeated. By 1945, Augusta had left New York City to live a presumably peaceful life in the Catskills region of New York State. It's not clear why or how she purchased a small farmhouse in the town of Saugerties, where she raised poultry and kept a garden. She also worked as a laboratory technician for a microbiologist and cancer researcher, Herman Knaust, whose family became her close friends and patrons. She continued to sculpt and maintained a studio in a former chicken coop. Her first commission in Saugerties, arranged for her by Herman Knaust, was a bust of Poultney Bigelow, a prolific author at that time in his nineties, who had known Kaiser Wilhelm II, Mark Twain, Frederic Remington, and Israel Zangwill. Augusta taught art in summer camps and at resorts on Martha's Vineyard. She made sculptures of the children in her community and recited poetry at community events. When Herman Knaust gave her a car, she learned to drive. Her house in Saugerties was on the bus route to New York City; friends and family visited often. In summers, her house became a summer camp for children of her Harlem friends. She wrote three texts for children's books, which were never published. She left few footprints. Irene had no children.

Although she was a beloved member of her community and is still remembered there with respect and affection, the community was very white. The road Augusta lived on was called Nigger Road, dating back to the nineteenth century, when it led to an encampment of Black road construction workers; she lived on that road for some twenty years. In the 1970s, several years after her death, a *g* was dropped and the pronunciation changed. In 1999, Karlyn Knaust Elia, Herman Knaust's daughter and the historian of the town of Saugerties, was instrumental in honoring Augusta by petitioning to officially have the road renamed. Augusta Savage Road was officially dedicated on April 5, 2000. The Knaust Elia family, the Saugerties Historical Society, and the town of Saugerties remembers her and keeps her house as a memorial.

ACKNOWLEDGMENTS

The author wishes to acknowledge the following publications, in which some of these poems first appeared, sometimes as earlier versions: Academy of American Poets' Poem-a-Day: "Crows"; *The Eloquent Poem*, edited by Elise Paschen: "Seventy"; *Colorado Review*: "A Gift to Be"; *The Golden Shovel Anthology*, edited by Peter Kahn, Ravi Shankar, and Patricia Smith: "Bird-Feeder"; *Poetry*: "Marcus Garvey Sits for a Bust," "Fingers Remember," and "Hitting Bottom"; and *World Make Way: New Poems Inspired by Art from The Metropolitan Museum of Art*, edited by Lee Bennett Hopkins: "Studio."

The author also thanks the following individuals, who enabled her to write several poems and to locate and obtain permission to publish some of the images included in this book. Thanks to sculptor Meredith Bergmann, historian Margaret Bond, historian Karlyn Knaust Elia, historian Jill Lepore, and penguin facilitator Tad Richards. Thanks to editors Holly Amos, Lindsay Garbutt, and Fred Sasaki, on the editorial and art staff of *Poetry*. And, for silent guidance, thanks to: the DuSable Museum of African American History, the New-York Historical Society Museum & Library, the Schomburg Center for Research in Black Culture, the Smithsonian's National Museum of African American History and Culture, and Chicago's South Side Community Art Center.

PHOTOGRAPHY CREDITS

—⟨⟨⟨◆⟩⟩⟩—

Portrait of a Baby, page xiv: 1942, terracotta, 10" x 8 ½" x 8", signed; courtesy of Michael Rosenfeld Gallery LLC, New York, NY.

Garden Figure, page 4: 1942, hydrostone plaster and metal, 20 ¾" x 16 ½" x 20"; Art and Artifacts Division, Schomburg Center for Research in Black Culture, New York Public Library, Astor, Lenox and Tilden Foundations. Photo by Michael Scott Johnson.

Girl with Pigtails, page 9: *Untitled (Girl with Pigtails)*, c. 1935, bronze mounted on painted wood base, 11 ⅜" x 9" x 7" overall; courtesy of Michael Rosenfeld Gallery LLC, New York, NY.

Augusta Savage, page 13: Photographs and Prints Division, Schomburg Center for Research in Black Culture, New York Public Library, Astor, Lenox and Tilden Foundations.

Lenox Avenue, page 21: Photographs and Prints Division, Schomburg Center for Research in Black Culture, New York Public Library, Astor, Lenox and Tilden Foundations.

Within thirty seconds' walk of the 135th Street branch of the New York Public Library, page 23: Photographs and Prints Division, Schomburg Center for Research in Black Culture, New York Public Library, Astor, Lenox and Tilden Foundations.

Garvey in regalia, page 24: Photographs and Prints Division, Schomburg Center for Research in Black Culture, New York Public Library, Astor, Lenox and Tilden Foundations.

Passport image, page 34: Photographs and Prints Division, Schomburg Center for Research in Black Culture, New York Public Library, Astor, Lenox and Tilden Foundations.

Gamin, page 37: Art and Artifacts Division, Schomburg Center for Research in Black Culture, New York Public Library, Astor, Lenox and Tilden Foundations.

Reclining Nude, page 40, Art and Artifacts Division, Schomburg Center for Research in Black Culture, New York Public Library, Astor, Lenox and Tilden Foundations.

Head of Unidentified Youth, page 47: Photographs and Prints Division, Schomburg Center for Research in Black Culture, New York Public Library, Astor, Lenox and Tilden Foundations.

Leonore, page 49: Art and Artifacts Division, Schomburg Center for Research in Black Culture, New York Public Library, Astor, Lenox and Tilden Foundations.

Harlem Community Art Center, page 53: The Miriam and Ira D. Wallach Division of Art, Prints and Photographs: Photography Collection, New York Public Library.

The Harp, page 54: Photographs and Prints Division, Schomburg Center for Research in Black Culture, New York Public Library, Astor, Lenox and Tilden Foundations.

Augusta Savage with two of her statuettes, page 56: Photographs and Prints Division, Schomburg Center for Research in Black Culture, New York Public Library, Astor, Lenox and Tilden Foundations.

Realization, page 59: Photographs and Prints Division, Schomburg Center for Research in Black Culture, New York Public Library, Astor, Lenox and Tilden Foundations.

Bust of James Weldon Johnson, page 61: Art and Artifacts Division, Schomburg Center for Research in Black Culture, New York Public Library, Astor, Lenox and Tilden Foundations.

After the Glory, page 66: Photographs and Prints Division, Schomburg Center for Research in Black Culture, New York Public Library, Astor, Lenox and Tilden Foundations.

The Harp at the World's Fair, page 69: Manuscripts and Archives Division, New York Public Library, Astor, Lenox and Tilden Foundations.

The Pugilist, page 73: Art and Artifacts Division, Schomburg Center for Research in Black Culture, New York Public Library, Astor, Lenox and Tilden Foundations.

Augusta Savage presenting model to Grover Whalen, page 75: Manuscripts and Archives Division, New York Public Library, Astor, Lenox and Tilden Foundations.

Minerva, page 76: Art and Artifacts Division, Schomburg Center for Research in Black Culture, New York Public Library, Astor, Lenox and Tilden Foundations.

Augusta Savage's home in Saugerties, New York, page 79: Knaust family collection, Saugerties, NY.

Laughing Boy, page 80: Art and Artifacts Division, Schomburg Center for Research in Black Culture, New York Public Library, Astor, Lenox and Tilden Foundations.

Poultney Bigelow, page 87: Knaust family collection, Saugerties, NY.

Genevieve Nelson, page 89: Art and Artifacts Division, Schomburg Center for Research in Black Culture, New York Public Library, Astor, Lenox and Tilden Foundations.

Penguin, page 90: Knaust family collection, Saugerties, NY.

Bas Relief of a Female Dancer, page 97: Art and Artifacts Division, Schomburg Center for Research in Black Culture, New York Public Library, Astor, Lenox and Tilden Foundations.